THE FASCINATING
ANIMAL
BOOK
FOR KIDS

THE FASCINATING
ANIMAL
BOOK
FOR KIDS

500
WILD FACTS!

GINJER L. CLARKE

ROCKRIDGE
PRESS

For general information on our other products and services or to obtain technical support, please contact our Customer Care Department within the United States at (866) 744-2665, or outside the United States at (510) 253-0500.

Rockridge Press publishes its books in a variety of electronic and print formats. Some content that appears in print may not be available in electronic books, and vice versa.

TRADEMARKS: Rockridge Press and the Rockridge Press logo are trademarks or registered trademarks of Callisto Media Inc. and/or its affiliates, in the United States and other countries, and may not be used without written permission. All other trademarks are the property of their respective owners. Rockridge Press is not associated with any product or vendor mentioned in this book.

Book Design: Creative Giant Inc.; Mike Thomas, Chris Dickey, and Dan Hosek
Art Producer: Maura Boland
Editors: Jeanine Le Ny and Eliza Kirby
Fact check: Rachel Bozek

Photo Credits: Shutterstock, iStock, Pexels, U.S. Fish and Wildlife Service, and the following:

Chapter 1:
Immortal Shots, Magda Elhers, Charles J Sharp, Andrey, SonNy cZ, Becker1999 from Grove City, Marcus Spiske, JJ Harrison, Bernard Gagnon, cloudzilla, travelwayoflife, Lukas Kloeppel, Michael Mwakalundwa, I, Brocken Inaglory, Sarah Zimmerman, Brett Sayles, Cliff, Arturo de Frias Marques, Fernando Revilla, Andrew Mercer, Derek Keats from Johannesburg, South Africa, Anass ERRIHANI, Trace Hudson, Alma, Skeeze, Benjamint444, Jeroen Kransen, Uwe Schmidt
Chapter 2:
Egor Kamelev, James Wheeler, Ghedoghedo, Muséum de Toulouse, Katja Schulz from Washington, D. C., USA, Zigah111, Thomas Schoch, Chris F, Geoff Gallice, B Kimmel, Ken and Nyetta, Hectonichus, Dinobass, Ca.garcia.s, Bernard DUPONT from FRANCE, Sputniktilt, fir0002/Flagstaffotos, Iwoelbern, Charles J Sharp, Bernard Gagnon, Doug Beckers from Macmasters Beach, Australia, Ilia Ustyantsev from Russia, Aaron Pomerantz, Nevit Dilmen, Javi Guerra Hernando, João P. Burini, Rison Thumboor from Thrissur India, Shamique, Marshal Hedin
Chapter 3:
Tom Fisk, Fox, Maky.Orel, George Desipris, Janne Hellsten from Helsinki, Finland, W.carter, Sheila Sund, Michael L. Baird, NASA, Whit Welles, Brocken Inaglory, Albert kok, Thomas Alexander, Hemming1952, Greg Skomal/NOAA Fisheries Service, Matthew Rader, Alexander Vasenin, Alexandro Rosa de Mello, Steve Childs, dro!d from atlanta, usa, Al Furkan
Chapter 4:
Henning Roettger, Charles J Sharp, Stu's Images, Congaree National Park from Hopkins, SC, USA, Thegreenj, Egor Kamelev, will, Peter Paplanus from St. Louis, Missouri, Betta.1, P.Lindgren
Chapter 5:
Gratisography, Darius Krause, Francisco Welter-Schultes, Artem Lysenko, Peter Paplanus from St. Louis, Missouri, Will Brown, Geoff Gallice from Gainesville, FL, B Kimmel, Justin Meissen, Rushenb, Lamiot
Chapter 6:
Kat Jayne, JJ Harrison, Drferry, Mwanner, Andreas Trepte, Olaf Oliviero Riemer, Christian Mehlführer, Eric Kilby from Somerville, MA, Naushil Ansari, H. Raab, Colin, Peterdownunder, Dr. Raju Kasambe, Seney Natural History Association, Charles J Sharp, Becky Matsubara from El Sobrante, California, Frank Cone, Monique Laats, Christopher Michel, Fernando Flores, Andreas Weith, Pedro Szekely from Los Angeles, CA

ISBN: Print 978-1-64611-149-7 | eBook 978-1-64611-150-3
R0

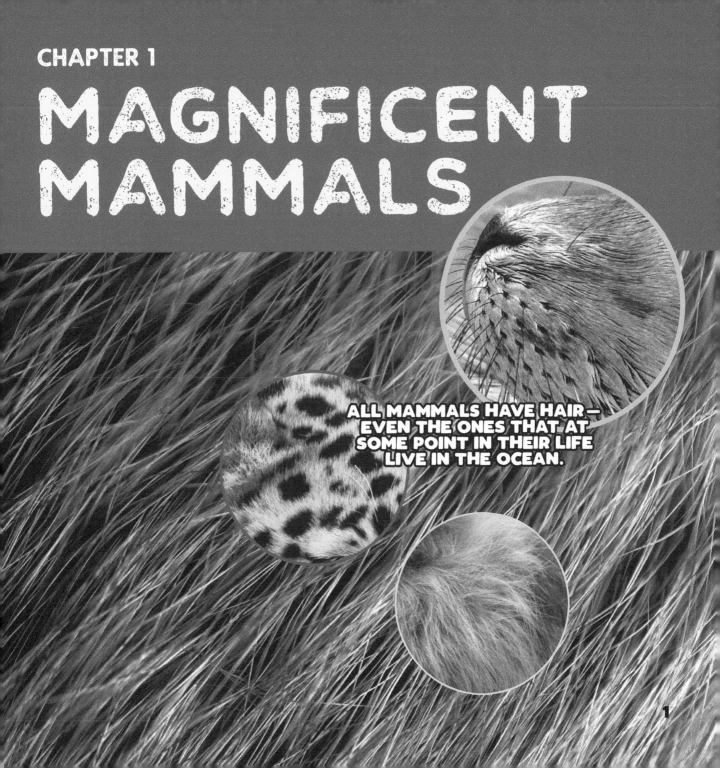

MAGNIFICENT MAMMALS

ALL MAMMALS HAVE HAIR—
EVEN THE ONES THAT AT
SOME POINT IN THEIR LIFE
LIVE IN THE OCEAN.

AWESOME ELEPHANTS

A MALE AFRICAN ELEPHANT is the largest land mammal, weighing up to **13,000 POUNDS (6,100 KG)—** that's as heavy as three SUVs.

AN ELEPHANT WALKS ON THE TIPS OF ITS TOES, LIKE A PERSON WALKING IN HIGH-HEELED SHOES.

ELEPHANTS CAN'T JUMP.

An elephant's **fabulous trunk** is powered by about **40,000** muscles.

A car could go **20 miles (32 km)** using the methane gas produced by one elephant's farts in a single day.

ELEPHANT RELATIVES

The itty-bitty 10-pound (4.5-kg) **ROCK HYRAX** is the closest relative to the elephant.

Like elephants, rock hyraxes have flat toenails and teeth that are

similar to tusks.

THE **ELEPHANT SHREW** HAS A TINY, TRUNK-LIKE SNOUT.

THE NOSE-Y **TAPIR** IS NOT RELATED TO THE ELEPHANT, BUT IT IS A RELATIVE OF BOTH HORSES AND RHINOCEROSES.

A **SAIGA ANTELOPE'S** FLOPPY NOSE POINTS DOWN AND KEEPS OUT DUST FROM THE DRY DESERT.

The **AARDVARK** gets its name from a South African word for "earth pig."

THE GIANT ANTEATER

is totally toothless. It slurps its food using its tongue, which can be up to

TWO FEET LONG.

Giant anteater

NOSES TO KNOW

BIG CATS

Female lion

A MALE LION sleeps up to 20 hours per day. **FEMALES** get less sleep, because they hunt for food and take care of the cubs.

A TIGER'S night vision is **SIX TIMES** better than a human's.

THE CHEETAH IS THE ONLY BIG CAT THAT CANNOT ROAR.

The **snow leopard** keeps warm by wrapping its long, fluffy tail around its body.

BLACK PANTHERS ARE NOT A SEPARATE SPECIES: THEY ARE DARK-COLORED LEOPARDS AND JAGUARS.

The JAGUAR'S name comes from the Native American word *yaguar*, which means "ONE WHO KILLS WITH A SINGLE LEAP."

NOT YOUR PET CAT

THE BEAUTIFUL **OCELOT** IS ABOUT A THIRD OF THE SIZE OF A LEOPARD AND TWICE AS BIG AS A HOUSE CAT.

The graceful **SERVAL** can leap up to 10 feet (3 m) into the air to catch a bird in flight.

The desert-dwelling SAND CAT can go for weeks without drinking water. Instead, its prey keeps it hydrated.

FISHING CATS have webbed front feet to help them swim and hunt.

The powerful
LYNX
may attack animals up to
FOUR TIMES
its own size.

MARVELOUS MARSUPIALS

Quokka

QUOKKAS
always appear to
be smiling. They're
even known as
**"THE
HAPPIEST
ANIMALS
ON EARTH."**

NUMBATS
EAT UP TO
20,000
TERMITES
EVERY DAY.

SUGAR GLIDERS
can soar over
150 feet (45.72 m)
between trees—
that's half the
length of a
football field.

THE TASMANIAN DEVIL
gets its name from the
SCARY SCREAM
it makes when it hunts at night.

THE WOMBAT
IS THE ONLY
ANIMAL IN THE
WORLD THAT
MAKES CUBE-
SHAPED POOP.

VIRGINIA OPOSSUM
BABIES ARE SO
SMALL THAT UP
TO 20 OF THEM
COULD FIT INTO
A TEASPOON.

11

Qiviut (KIV-ee-oot) is the super-soft, ultra-warm belly wool of the **musk ox**.

WEIRD ANIMAL

A baby **platypus** is called a **puggle**.

12

The big, twisting hop a **rabbit** takes when it's excited is called a **binky**— like a child's pacifier.

WORDS

Pronking is when a **gazelle** leaps high into the air with all four feet at once.

Guano is another name for **bat** poop.

HUNGRY, HUNGRY HIPPO?

The **HIPPO** oozes an oily, red liquid that acts as **SUNSCREEN** for its two-inch-thick skin.

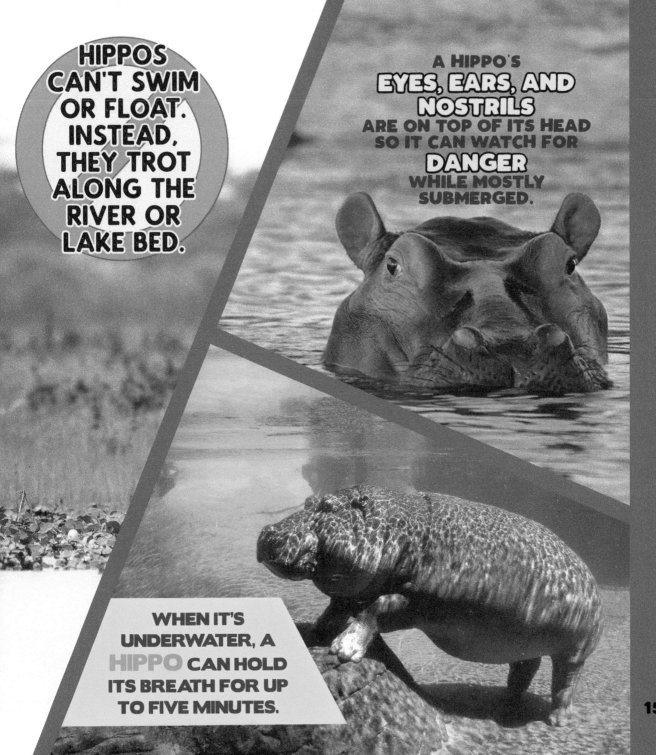

HIPPOS CAN'T SWIM OR FLOAT. INSTEAD, THEY TROT ALONG THE RIVER OR LAKE BED.

A HIPPO'S **EYES, EARS, AND NOSTRILS** ARE ON TOP OF ITS HEAD SO IT CAN WATCH FOR **DANGER** WHILE MOSTLY SUBMERGED.

WHEN IT'S UNDERWATER, A **HIPPO** CAN HOLD ITS BREATH FOR UP TO FIVE MINUTES.

HORNED HEADS

THE YAK'S shaggy coat protects it from the **EXTREME COLD.**

THE **CAPE BUFFALO** HAS ITS OWN BUG EXTERMINATORS. OXPECKERS EAT THE FLEAS, TICKS, AND LICE LIVING IN ITS FUR.

A male **BIGHORN SHEEP'S** horns weigh up to 30 pounds (13 kg), which can be more than the rest of his skeleton.

A **RHINOCEROS HORN** is made of keratin, also found in human hair.

SUPER STRIPES

With small horns and a long, bluish tongue, the **OKAPI** is the giraffe's only close relative.

BONGOS only come out of the forest at night— to visit natural **SALT LICKS**, their favorite treat.

Female and young male **NYALAS** have stripes, but adult males do not.

ZEBRA SKIN IS **BLACK** UNDER ALL THOSE **STRIPES**.

GENTLE, GIANT GIRAFFES

A BABY **GIRAFFE** IS 6 FEET (1.8 M) TALL AT BIRTH AND CAN STAND UP ALMOST IMMEDIATELY.

THE GIRAFFE is the tallest land mammal at **17 FEET (5.3 M)**– about as tall as three stacked refrigerators.

GIRAFFES ARE USUALLY VERY QUIET, BUT SOMETIMES THEY MAKE LOW HUMMING SOUNDS AT NIGHT.

Every **GIRAFFE** has a unique pattern of spots, so no two giraffes look exactly the same.

Giraffes **are born with ossicones, which look like small horns.**

POPPIN' UP EVERYWHERE

A group of **MEERKATS** is called a mob.

When two **PRAIRIE DOGS** first meet, they lock teeth, and it looks like they're kissing.

Groundhogs named Punxsutawney Phil have been "predicting" the weather on Groundhog Day since February 2, 1887.

FEELING SQUIRRELLY?

Tree squirrels can climb headfirst both up and down trees because their back legs are double-jointed and they have very sharp claws.

Like all rodents, a SQUIRREL's teeth never stop growing.

THERE ARE 200 TYPES OF SQUIRRELS. THEY CAN BE FOUND ON ALL CONTINENTS EXCEPT FOR AUSTRALIA AND ANTARCTICA.

21

LITTLE CUTIES

Jerboa

A NEWBORN EASTERN CHIPMUNK WEIGHS ONLY ONE-TENTH OF AN OUNCE (3 G)—A LITTLE MORE THAN A PENNY.

EACH CHINCHILLA HAIR FOLLICLE MAY GROW UP TO **50 HAIRS** AT ONCE.

THE JERBOA LIVES IN THE GOBI DESERT AND NEVER DRINKS WATER—IT HYDRATES THROUGH THE PLANTS AND INSECTS IT EATS.

Today's HAMSTERS are all descendants of a single hamster family that lived in Syria around 1930.

PRETTY IN PINK

The **star-nosed mole** has 22 **pink feelers** on its nose to help it find its way in the dark.

Star-nosed mole

THE NAKED MOLE RAT QUEEN IS THE ONLY MEMBER OF THE COLONY THAT PRODUCES BABIES.

THE PINK FAIRY ARMADILLO is pink because blood vessels show through ITS THIN SHELL.

CAN YOU BEAR IT?

THE GIANT PANDA HAS THE BIGGEST MOLARS OF ANY MAMMAL–IT USES THEM TO EAT CRUNCHY BAMBOO.

During hibernation, **BLACK BEARS** can go for up to 100 days without food or water.

A KODIAK BEAR CAN BE 10 FEET (3 M) TALL STANDING UPRIGHT.

The **RED PANDA** is related to raccoons, not bears, and it is nocturnal like its cousins.

A POLAR BEAR CAN SMELL PREY, LIKE A SEAL, FROM 20 MILES (32 KM) AWAY AND THROUGH THICK ICE.

HANGIN' AROUND

A **SLOTH** EATS, SLEEPS, PEES, AND EVEN GIVES BIRTH HANGING UPSIDE DOWN IN A TREE.

THE **BUSH BABY** DOES NOT HAVE EYE SOCKETS, SO IT MOVES ITS HEAD CONSTANTLY WHILE IT HUNTS FOR FOOD.

A male
RING-TAILED LEMUR
rubs his tail on his stinky scent glands, and then waves it to warn away rivals.

The name KOALA comes from an Aboriginal word meaning "no water" because the koala gets most of its water from eucalyptus leaves.

27

GOING BATTY

BATS ARE THE ONLY FLYING MAMMALS.

Most bats can't walk because their leg bones are too thin.

SOME BATS CAN EAT THEIR OWN WEIGHT IN INSECTS—IN ONE NIGHT.

A VAMPIRE BAT
doesn't suck blood; it uses its tongue
TO LAP BLOOD
from a small cut in its victim's skin.

FLYING FOXES ARE THE LARGEST BATS IN THE WORLD, WITH WINGSPANS OF UP TO 6 FEET (1.8 M).

Flying fox

The smallest bat—and mammal—in the world is the **BUMBLEBEE BAT**. It weighs less than a penny.

WATER RATS

NUTRIA HAVE GIANT FRONT TEETH THAT ARE **BRIGHT ORANGE** AND STRONG BECAUSE THEY CONTAIN IRON.

A single **BEAVER** can cut down 200 trees in one year.

THE **CAPYBARA** IS THE WORLD'S LARGEST RODENT, WEIGHING UP TO 175 POUNDS (79 KG).

FEELING FOXY

The **BAT-EARED FOX**'s huge ears help it keep cool and detect underground insects.

IF AN ARCTIC FOX RUNS OUT OF FOOD, IT WILL EAT A POLAR BEAR'S LEFTOVERS.

The FENNEC FOX has fur on the bottoms of its paws to protect it from the HOT DESERT SAND.

AMAZING ANTLERS

In Alaska, there are
MORE CARIBOU THAN PEOPLE.

Caribou herd

While a MOOSE'S ANTLERS are growing, they are covered with a soft skin called VELVET.

MALE ELKS MAKE A GRUNTING SOUND THAT ENDS IN A HIGH-PITCHED WHISTLE. THIS IS CALLED BUGLING.

REINDEER mostly eat lichen— also called REINDEER MOSS— which is shaped like tiny antlers.

ALL IN THE FAMILY

BACTRIAN CAMELS HAVE TWO HUMPS, WHILE DROMEDARIES HAVE ONE.

At one time, **ONLY ROYALTY** was allowed to wear the **FLUFFY FLEECE** of an **ALPACA.**

THE **CAMEL'S** AMAZING EYELASHES HELP KEEP DESERT SAND FROM BLOWING INTO ITS EYES.

Andean people have raised **llamas** for their wool for thousands of years.

HOWL
ARE YOU?

GRAY WOLVES HOWL TO COMMUNICATE WITH EACH OTHER AND — SOMETIMES — TO MAKE THEIR PACK SOUND BIGGER.

Gray wolf

COYOTES USE MANY DIFFERENT SOUNDS TO COMMUNICATE.

The **MANED WOLF** has very long legs so it can see over the tall African savanna grasses.

36

DON'T MESS WITH US

When threatened, the **SPOTTED SKUNK** does a handstand and sprays a nasty-smelling liquid from its rear.

WOLVERINES KEEP ANIMALS AWAY FROM THEIR KILL BY **GROWLING** WITH BARED TEETH AND SHOWING THEIR RAZOR-SHARP CLAWS.

The **HONEY BADGER** often raids honeybee nests and can survive many bee stings.

WHILE **HYENAS** SOMETIMES CHASE LIONS AWAY FROM THEIR OWN KILLS, THEY ARE ALSO VERY GOOD HUNTERS.

37

PLEASE DON'T TOUCH

THE HEDGEHOG

got its name because it grunts like a pig as it digs in the hedges for insects.

38

THE PANGOLIN ROLLS INTO A TIGHT BALL WHEN IT SENSES TROUBLE AND IS ALMOST IMPOSSIBLE FOR PEOPLE TO UNROLL.

The ECHIDNA, or spiny anteater, is one of only two egg-laying mammals.

EACH BARBED QUILL ON AN AFRICAN PORCUPINE CAN BE UP TO 1 FOOT (30.5 CM) LONG.

39

MISCHIEVOUS MONKEYS

JAPANESE MACAQUES, OR SNOW MONKEYS, SOMETIMES STAY WARM AND RELAX BY LOUNGING IN VOLCANIC HOT SPRING POOLS.

The HOWLER MONKEY's booming call can be heard 3 miles (4.8 km) away.

Red uakari

THE RED UAKARI'S BRIGHT RED FACE MEANS IT'S HEALTHY, NOT EMBARRASSED. SICK UAKARIS HAVE PALE FACES.

Capuchin monkeys are very clever and can be trained as service animals.

GOLDEN LION TAMARIN mothers usually give birth twice a year—and they always have twins.

41

ABSOLUTELY APE

THE WESTERN LOWLAND GORILLA'S OFFICIAL SCIENTIFIC NAME IS *GORILLA GORILLA GORILLA*.

THE WORLD'S LARGEST TREE MAMMAL, THE ORANGUTAN, BUILDS SLEEPING NESTS AS HIGH AS 65 FEET (20 M) OFF THE GROUND.

Western lowland gorilla

THE SIAMANG GIBBON CAN PUFF OUT ITS THROAT SAC WHEN IT'S MAKING SOUNDS— IT CAN ENLARGE TO BE THE SIZE OF A HUMAN HEAD.

CHIMPANZEES can learn hundreds of words in sign language and can communicate with humans.

CHAPTER 2

CREEPY CRAWLIES

ABOUT 80 PERCENT OF ALL CREATURES ON EARTH ARE INSECTS.

ANCIENT INSECT

MEGANEURA, a giant ancient dragonfly, had a wingspan of almost 30 inches (76 cm). That's about the length of an adult human's leg.

FASTEST FLYERS

DRAGONFLIES ARE THE FASTEST-FLYING INSECTS AT 35 MILES (56 KM) PER HOUR—FASTER THAN THE BEST HUMAN RUNNERS.

DRAGONFLIES **HAVE WINGSPANS BETWEEN 2 AND 5 INCHES (5 AND 13 CM).**

A **DRAGONFLY** only eat the prey it cat in flight.

SOME DRAGONFLIES can spend years **IN THE WATER AS LARVAE,** but live only a few weeks as flying adults.

LONGEST JUMPER

Some fleas jump more than

150 TIMES

their height.

MMM, TASTY BUGS

Around 2,000 insect species are considered **edible** for humans.

Fried crickets

MILITARY SURVIVAL MANUALS INCLUDE INSTRUCTIONS TO EAT INSECTS IF NO OTHER FOOD IS AVAILABLE.

PEOPLE IN AUSTRALIA SAY THAT WITCHETTY GRUBS TASTE LIKE CHICKEN OR FRIED EGGS.

Insects are a
GREAT SOURCE OF PROTEIN—
from roasted grubs to fried crickets to
SCORPIONS ON A STICK.

BLOODSUCKERS

THE HIRUDO LEECH HAS THREE JAWS AND AT LEAST 200 TEETH.

Leeches have been used in medicine for over 2,500 years.

A leech has at least **32** brains.

These SLIMY SUPERSTARS help wounds heal by getting rid of old blood to make room for new healthy blood.

Leeches raised in laboratories often feed on
SHEEP'S BLOOD.

SLUG-TASTIC

THE MASCOT OF THE UNIVERSITY OF CALIFORNIA SANTA CRUZ IS THE BANANA SLUG.

Some **SEA SLUGS** e
jellyfish tentacles a
store their stinging
inside their bodies t
against predators.

A **SLUG** has
four tentacles
which it uses
see and sme

SQUIRMY WORMS

Earthworms need oxygen, but they don't have lungs—they breathe through their skin.

THE MEGURO PARASITOLOGICAL MUSEUM IS HOME TO WHAT IS POSSIBLY THE WORLD'S LONGEST TAPEWORM—A WORM THAT LIVES INSIDE OF OTHER CREATURES. IT'S 28 FEET (8.8 M) LONG.

Velvet worm

The **VELVET WORM** squirts a sticky substance from two openings on its head to catch its prey.

THE LARGEST OF THEM ALL

THE GIANT AFRICAN SNAIL EATS THE PAINT OFF HOUSES TO HELP GROW ITS BASEBALL-SIZED SHELL.

The **GOLIATH BEETLE**, one of the world's heaviest insects, weighs up to 3.5 ounces (100 g)—about the weight of a deck of cards.

The giant centipede has very fast feet and venomous claws—all the better to hunt with.

The **GIANT WĒTĀPUNGA** sheds 11 exoskeletons before becoming an adult.

BUNCHES OF BEETLES

MORE THAN 350,000 SPECIES OF **BEETLES** HAVE BEEN DISCOVERED— SO FAR.

LONGHORN BEETLES DON'T HAVE HORNS, BUT THEIR ANTENNAE CAN BE FIVE TIMES LONGER THAN THEIR BODIES.

The male **RHINOCEROS BEETLE** is known for its giant horn and is sometimes called a **UNICORN BEETLE**.

MALE STAG BEETLES fight with their **JAWS** the same way stags use their antlers.

DUNG BEETLES ROLL ANIMAL POOP INTO BALLS AND THEN EAT IT OR LAY THEIR EGGS IN IT. SOME BALLS CAN BE AS BIG AS AN APPLE.

The SCARAB BEETLES featured in ancient Egyptian art are actually dung beetles that symbolize the sun.

MAKE SOME NOISE

A HARLEQUIN BUG SQUEAKS LOUDLY.

The Madagascar hissing cockroach **makes a loud sound when it breathes.**

EVEN WHEN THE MALE MOLE CRICKET IS UNDERGROUND, HIS CHIRPING CALL IS LOUD ENOUGH FOR FEMALES TO HEAR ON THE SURFACE.

KATYDIDS play a summertime song with their wings that sounds as if they are saying "zip" and "ze

CYCLICAL CICADAS

LE CICADAS make noise with
s called tymbals, which are at the
m of their abdomen. Females
much quieter noises than
, by flicking their wings.

**CICADAS ARE
MONG THE LOUDEST
ECTS IN THE WORLD.
HEIR SOUNDS CAN
ACH 108 DECIBELS—
OSE TO THE VOLUME
OF A JET PLANE
TAKING OFF.**

**BABY CICADAS,
CALLED NYMPHS,
DRINK SAP FROM
TREE ROOTS.**

**Some cicadas burrow
underground to grow,
then emerge as adults
17 years later.**

EARTHQUAKE!

Some ants can sense whe[n] **EARTHQUA[KE]** is coming, so they [come] out of their burr[ows].

SUPER SWARMS

Farmers fear **LOCUSTS**— a swarm can eat **HUNDREDS OF TONS** of corn or wheat every day.

mmer, there are more
OSQUITOES
Arctic tundra than anywhere else
THE WORLD.

PERFECT PREDATORS

Tiny but mighty

BULLDOG ANTS

have venom strong enough to

KILL HUMANS.

WHEN ASIAN GIANT HORNETS RAID A HONEYBEE HIVE, THEY BITE OFF THE ADULT BEES' HEADS.

The GIANT WATER BUG is 4 inches (10.2 cm) long, with large pincers and a venomous bite.

PRAYING MANTISES ARE CANNIBALS. THE FEMALES OFTEN EAT THEIR MATES, AND BABIES SOMETIMES EAT THEIR SIBLINGS.

The TARANTULA HAWK WASP lays her eggs on a tarantula she has stung. When the baby wasp hatches, it eats the paralyzed spider.

HAPPY HOPPERS

The **CAMEL CRICKET,** also known as the cave cricket, jumps to escape predators, but it also sometimes jumps *at* them.

LEAFHOPPERS EAT PLANTS BUT SOMETIMES ALSO KILL THEM — THEY ARE KNOWN TO INJECT A TOXIN INTO PLANTS AS THEY EAT.

In a field during summer, one square yard (0.84 sq m) can hold **20 GRASSHOPPERS.**

COOL CAMOUFLAGE

Leaf insects blend in with leaves—nymphs even sway slightly to look like leaves in the wind.

SPECIES OF **WALKING**
K, WHICH BLENDS IN
H PLANTS, CAN
W TO ALMOST
ET (61 CM) LONG.

THORN BUGS, ALSO CALLED TREEHOPPERS, HIDE FROM PREDATORS BY LOOKING LIKE THORNS ON BRANCHES.

THE PEPPERED MOTH CATERPILLAR changes its appearance to match the twig it sits on.

LIGHTS IN THE NIGHT

FIREFLIES USE THEIR LIGHTS TO TALK TO EACH OTHER. EACH SPECIES HAS A UNIQUE FLASHING PATTERN.

THE RAILROAD WORM, sometimes called the glowworm, has a glowing red head and two lines of yellowish-green dots on its sides.

Cave-dwelling **GLOWWORMS** lure insects into their sticky string traps with a glowing tail light.

SOME CLICK BEETLES HAVE "HEADLIGHTS"—TWO GLOWING SPOTS ON THEIR HEADS—BUT UNLIKE FIREFLIES, THEY DON'T BLINK.

BUGS THAT HELP

ybees make about **10 MILLION** trips
en flowers and their hive to collect enough nectar to make
NE POUND OF HONEY.

It takes about 2,0
**SILKWOR
COCOO**
to make one po
of

THE LADYBUG EATS UP TO
5,000 APHIDS IN ITS LIFETIME.

HORRIBLE HAWK MOTH

The **DEATH'S HEAD HAWK MOTH** has a skull-shaped marking on its back.

a hawk moth caterpillar is ...tened, it puffs up its head to look like a ...iper, which scares its attacker.

In the 1800s, people believed seeing this harmless moth was a **BAD OMEN.**

MARVELOUS MOTHS

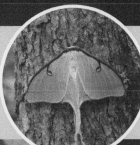

Atlas moth

THE **HUMMINGBIRD MOTH** flies quickly and has a long nectar-sucking proboscis that looks like a hummingbird beak.

THE COLORFUL ATLAS MOTH'S WINGSPAN CAN BE AS BIG AS A DINNER PLATE— UP TO 12 INCHES (30 CM) ACROSS.

BEAUTIFUL BUTTERFLIES

Queen Alexandra's birdwing

The largest butterfly is the **QUEEN ALEXANDRA'S BIRDWING.** Females have a wingspan of about 12 inches (30 cm).

EVERY AUTUMN, MILLIONS OF **MONARCH BUTTERFLIES** MIGRATE UP TO **3,000 MILES** (4,828 KM) TO CALIFORNIA OR MEXICO.

The smallest butter[fly] is the half-inch (1.3-c[m]) western pygmy blue.

The **BLUE MORPHO** butterfly is brown when its wings are closed but a spectacular blue when its wings are open.

MOST VENOMOUS SPIDERS

THE FEMALE **BLACK WIDOW** SPIDER'S VENOM IS 15 TIMES STRONGER THAN A RATTLESNAKE'S.

Female black widow

Male
black widow

**THE DEADLY
BRAZILIAN WANDERING SPIDER**
DOES NOT BUILD A WEB OR NEST TO
CATCH PREY; INSTEAD, IT HUNTS BY
WANDERING THE FOREST FLOOR.

The shy but dang
BROWN RECLU
is the size of a quarter and
violin-shaped mark on its

HAIRY HUNTERS

The **HUNTSMAN SPIDER** scurries from side to side like a crab before quickly grabbing its prey.

The **GOLIATH BIRD-EATING SPIDER** flings tiny hairs from its back at predators to cause a burning sensation and even **blindness.**

TRUE TARANTULAS LIVE ONLY IN SOUTHERN EUROPE.

TRICKY SPIDERS

Ant-eating, ANT-MIMICKING spiders pretend to be ants by raising two of their eight legs so they look like ant antennae.

A FISHING SPIDER can stay underwater for 30 minutes while it waits for its fish prey.

THE TRAPDOOR SPIDER builds a silken door for its burrow and lays trip lines outside, which signal when prey is within grabbing distance.

WONDERFUL WEBS

THE GOLDEN ORB-WEAVER USES ITS SEVEN TYPES OF SILK GLANDS TO BUILD WEBS, MAKE EGG CASES, AND WRAP UP PREY.

The BOLAS SPIDER uses a strand of silk with a sticky end to "fish" for insects.

A female TRASHLINE ORB-WEAVER places poop and bits of trash in her web, then hides with her egg cases among the assortment of junk.

DEADLY
SCORPIONS

The **DESERT HAIRY SCORPION** is the largest scorpion in North America.

DURING THE DAY, SCORPIONS BLEND WITH THEIR SURROUNDINGS, BUT IF YOU SHINE A UV LIGHT ON THEM, THEY GLOW IN THE DARK.

Male **BLACK EMPEROR SCORPIONS** will fight to the death over their territory.

THE DEATHSTALKER IS DANGEROUS SCORPIOI BUT SCIENTISTS ARE US ITS VENOM FOR SOMETH GOOD: CANCER RESEARC

HEY, COUSIN!

A DADDY LONGLEGS MAY *LOOK* LIKE A SPIDER, BUT IT'S ACTUALLY A RELATIVE OF THE SCORPION.

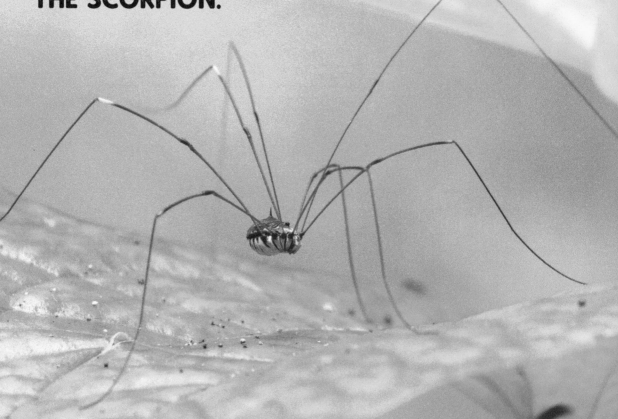

CHAPTER 3
WATER WORLD

THERE ARE MORE THAN
33,000 SPECIES OF FISH—
MORE THAN ALL BIRDS, MAMMALS,
AND REPTILES COMBINED.

JUST JELLIES

MOON JELLYFISH WERE ABOARD THE SPACE SHUTTLE *COLUMBIA* SO SCIENTISTS COULD STUDY HOW JELLYFISH GROW WITHOUT GRAVITY.

JELLYFISH ARE 95 PERCENT WATER AND HAVE NO BRAIN, HEART, OR BONES.

The **IMMORTAL JELLYFISH** can live forever. It grows to adulthood then reverts back to being a baby, over and over again.

BEAUTIFUL BUT DEADLY

GROUPS OF GIANT NOMURA'S JELLYFISH ARE SOMETIMES SO LARGE THAT THEY CLOG UP NUCLEAR POWER PLANTS AND FORCE THEM TO SHUT DOWN.

Nomura's jellyfish

THE PORTUGUESE MAN O' WAR HAS ENOUGH VENOM TO INSTANTLY PARALYZE OR KILL ITS PREY.

THE VENOM IN A BOX JELLYFISH'S STING IS 100 TIMES STRONGER THAN A KING COBRA'S BITE.

THE LION'S MANE JELLYFISH HAS 800 TENTACLES, SOME OF WHICH CAN BE MORE THAN 100 FEET (30 M) LONG.

TRASHY ART

To raise awareness about ocean pollution, an Oregon artist created **HUGE SEA CREATURE SCULPTURES** made out of plastic found on the beach.

The UNICORN SHRIMP's horn is alled a rostrum, and has a jagged surface that looks like tiny teeth.

The **goblin shark**'s pointy snout works like an antenna—it receives electric signals from fish it will hunt.

UNDERWATER UNICORNS

AS IT MATURES, THE WHITEMARGIN UNICORNFISH GROWS A BONY HORN ON ITS HEAD.

The male **NARWHAL**'s long, spiral tusk is really a **TOOTH** growing out of its top lip. It has only one other tooth inside its mouth.

SILLY SHRIMP

SOME MANTIS SHRIMP ARE STRONG ENOUGH TO BREAK AQUARIUM GLASS WITH THEIR LIGHTNING-FAST PUNCHES.

FUNNY FACES

RED-LIPPED BATFISH CAN WALK ON THE OCEAN FLOOR WITH SPECIAL FINS.

The **deep-sea blobfish** was once voted the ugliest animal on Earth by the Ugly Animal Preservation Society.

Sea lamprey

THE **SEA LAMPREY**'S MOUTH IS FILLED WITH **SHARP TEETH** THAT LATCH ONTO PREY AS IT SUCKS OUT ITS VICTIM'S BLOOD AND BODY FLUIDS.

MAMA MANATEE

A BABY MANATEE IS BORN UNDERWATER AND THEN LEARNS TO SWIM FROM ITS MOTHER—IN ABOUT AN HOUR.

SUPER SWIMMERS

SEA OTTER
skin has up to
ONE MILLION
hairs per square inch. This dense fur keeps these animals warm and dry.

A **SEA OTTER** PUP CAN FLOAT, BUT IT CAN'T SWIM, SO IT SLEEPS ON ITS MOTHER'S BELLY.

SEA OTTER poop is called **SPRAINT**, and it smells like herbal tea.

93

FUNNY FEET

Seals, sea lions, and walruses belong to a group called **PINNIPEDS**, which means **"FINNED FEET."**

THE **WALRUS'S** SCIENTIFIC NAME MEANS **"TOOTH-WALKING SEA HORSE"** BECAUSE IT USES ITS LONG TUSKS TO CLIMB OUT OF THE WATER.

A WALRUS can sleep for 19 hours, but it can also stay awake for more than **THREE DAYS** when it's out hunting.

WACKY
WALRUSES

ENORMOUS ELEPHANT SEALS

THE MALE ELEPHANT SEAL'S SNOUT IS CALLED A **PROBOSCIS** (PRO-BAHS-KISS) AND MAY BE OVER A FOOT LONG.

Adult male
ELEPHANT SEALS
can be 20 feet (6.1 m) long and weigh
8,800 POUNDS (4,000 kg)—
sometimes eight times bigger than female elephant seals.

ELEPHANT SEALS
dive as deep as 1 mile (1.6 km)
to hunt squid—and may stay
down for up to two hours.

SO MANY SEALS!

ABOUT 15 MILLION CRABEATER SEALS LIVE IN THE ANTARCTIC OCEAN. THE ONLY LARGE ANIMALS WITH A BIGGER POPULATION ON THE PLANET ARE HUMANS.

THE LEOPARD SEAL IS A FIERCE PENGUIN PREDATOR IN THE WATER, BUT IT CAN'T CATCH ONE ON LAND.

Like whales, SEALS store energy in a thick layer of fat called blubber.

Harp seal

A HARP SEAL MOTHER CAN TELL WHICH SEAL PUP IS HERS BY ITS SMELL.

SEA DOGS

CALIFORNIA SEA LIONS
ARE FAMOUS FOR BARKING LIKE
DOGS, BUT THEY ALSO GRUNT,
GROWL, SQUEAL, TRUMPET,
BLEAT, AND BURP.

RIVER MERMAID

The **AMAZON RIVER DOLPHIN** is pink. It gets **PINKER** as it ages.

SEA SURFERS

WHEN A DOLPHIN SNOOZES, ONLY HALF OF ITS BRAIN GOES TO SLEEP. THIS ALLOWS IT TO KEEP SURFACING TO BREATHE.

Some dolphins use **SEA SPONGES** to protect their noses from sharp rocks and dangerous animals like sea urchins as they search for food.

BABY DOLPHINS have hair on their faces when they're born, but it quickly falls out.

A bottlenose dolphin using echolocation makes 1,000 CLICKING NOISES per second.

KILLER WHALE?

ORCAS ARE ACTUALLY
NOT WHALES AT ALL.
THEY'RE THE LARGEST MEMBERS
OF THE DOLPHIN FAMILY.

THE ORCA is the fastest sea mammal and can swim at speeds of up to **34 MILES** (55 km) per hour.

SAILORS ORIGINALLY GAVE ORCAS THE NICKNAME "WHALE KILLER" BECAUSE ORCAS HUNT WHALES.

WONDERFUL WHALES

BLUE WHALES ARE THE LARGEST ANIMALS ON THE PLANET.

BLUE WHALES can grow up to **100 FEET** (30 m) long and weigh **170 TONS.**

Scientists can estimate how old a **WHALE** is by how much ear wax it has.

HUMPBACK WHALES are known for singing complex, high-pitched songs that last up to 30 minutes.

Blue whale

A BELUGA WHALE IS ALL WHITE TO BLEND IN WITH ITS ICY HABITAT.

ANCIENT SHARKS

SHARKS were swimming the seas before dinosaurs roamed the Earth.

MEGALODON, meaning "giant tooth," was the largest shark that ever lived. It was 60 feet (18 m) long—possibly larger.

The largest **MEGALODON** tooth ever found is about three times larger than a present-day great white shark tooth.

SOME ANCIENT PEOPLE BELIEVED **MEGALODON** TEETH WERE SERPENT TONGUES THAT HAD TURNED TO STONE.

DID YOU KNOW?

Sharks never need to visit a dentist. Their teeth never get cavities.

While sharks do rest, experts believe that they don't sleep like humans do.

DEADLY SHARKS

THE HAMMERHEAD SHARK

knows how to use its head—to hold prey against the
seafloor before eating it.

TIGER SHARKS ARE SO AGGRESSIVE THAT THE BABIES MAY EAT ONE ANOTHER BEFORE THEY ARE BORN.

THE THRESHER SHARK STUNS PREY BY WHIPPING IT WITH ITS FANTASTICALLY LONG TAIL.

GREAT WHITE SHARKS HAVE BIG APPETITES, BUT THEY CAN GO MONTHS OR POSSIBLY A YEAR WITHOUT EATING.

HUGE SHARKS

The 50-foot-long (15 m) **WHALE SHARK** is the largest fish. It is longer than a tractor-trailer truck.

THE **GREENLAND SHARK** IS THE SLOWEST-MOVING FISH. IT SWIMS MORE SLOWLY THAN AN AVERAGE PERSON WALKS.

THE **BASKING SHARK** FILTERS 2,000 TONS OF WATER PER HOUR TO CATCH PLANKTON WITHIN ITS GILLS.

SMALL SHARKS

The **DWARF LANTERN SHARK** is usually 6 to 8 inches (15 to 20 cm) long and has glowing lights on its body that attract prey in the dark.

The **SPOTTED WOBBEGONG's** "beard" looks like seaweed. Confused prey swim right up to its mouth.

The
COOKIE CUTTER SHARK
takes perfectly round bites—just like a cookie cutter—out of big fish and other sharks.

111

FEARSOME FISH

THE BEAUTIFUL **LIONFISH** HAS VENOMOUS SPINES ON ITS BACK THAT CAN PARALYZE A PREDATOR.

THE GARFISH HAS GREEN BONES.

THE HAGFISH, OR SLIME EEL, TIES ITS BONELESS BODY INTO A KNOT TO INCREASE ITS BITING FORCE.

PIRANHA feed in groups and can devour a large fish or mammal in as little as a minute or two.

Watch where you step! STONEFISH are the most venomous fish in the sea and look like ordinary rocks on the seafloor.

The ANGLERFISH uses a glowing light on its head like a fishing pole to lure fish close—then snags them with its fangs.

BIG MAMA

THE ENORMOUS FEMALE OCEAN SUNFISH CAN PRODUCE UP TO 300 MILLION EGGS AT ONE TIME.

SKATES AND RAYS

SKATES AND STINGRAYS LOOK SIMILAR, BUT SKATES LAY EGG CASES AND STINGRAYS GIVE BIRTH TO LIVE BABIES.

DENTISTS IN ANCIENT GREECE SOMETIMES USED STINGRAY SPINE VENOM TO NUMB PATIENTS' MOUTHS.

SKATE EGG CASES are sometimes called mermaids' purses.

Manta ray

The manta ray has giant, bat-like fins that are 22 feet (6.7 m) wide— about the same width as a small plane's wingspan.

115

EERIE EELS

THE **GREEN MORAY EEL**, WHICH CAN GROW TO BE 8 FEET (2.4 M) LONG, HAS BEEN MISTAKEN FOR A MYTHOLOGICAL SEA SERPENT.

Green moray eel

The female **EUROPEAN EEL** migrates from Europe to the Sargasso Sea to lay her eggs—then her baby eels drift back on their own.

AN **ELECTRIC EEL** CAN STUN ITS PREY WITH 600 VOLTS. THAT'S ABOUT 50 TIMES MORE POWER THAN A CAR BATTERY.

Electric eel

THE **GULPER EEL** HAS AN ENORMOUS HINGED MOUTH TO SWALLOW ANIMALS BIGGER THAN ITSELF.

DOUBLE TROUBLE

THE **BLUE-RINGED OCTOPUS** IS BOTH **VENOMOUS** (THROUGH ITS BITE) AND **POISONOUS** (WHEN IT IS SWALLOWED).

GIANTS OF THE DEEP

One eyeball of a **GIANT SQUID** is bigger than a human head.

THE GIANT OCTOPUS SOMETIMES EATS ITS OWN ARMS.

The 56-foot-long (17-m) **OARFISH** is the world's longest bony fish—and has rarely been spotted alive.

FEELING CRABBY?

HORSESHOE CRABS are related to spiders, not crabs, and have looked the same for at least 300 million years.

Cold-water lobsters have front claws, while warm-water lobsters like the Caribbean spiny lobster do not.

120

THE **JAPANESE SPIDER CRAB** IS THE LARGEST CRAB, MEASURING 12 FEET (3.8 M) FROM CLAW TO CLAW.

IF A MALE **FIDDLER CRAB** LOSES HIS BIG CLAW, THE SMALLER CLAW GROWS TO THE SIZE OF THE ONE HE LOST.

OCEAN TRICKSTERS

The
DECORATOR CRAB
sticks bits of seaweed, sponges, and coral on its shell for the
ULTIMATE CAMOUFLAGE.

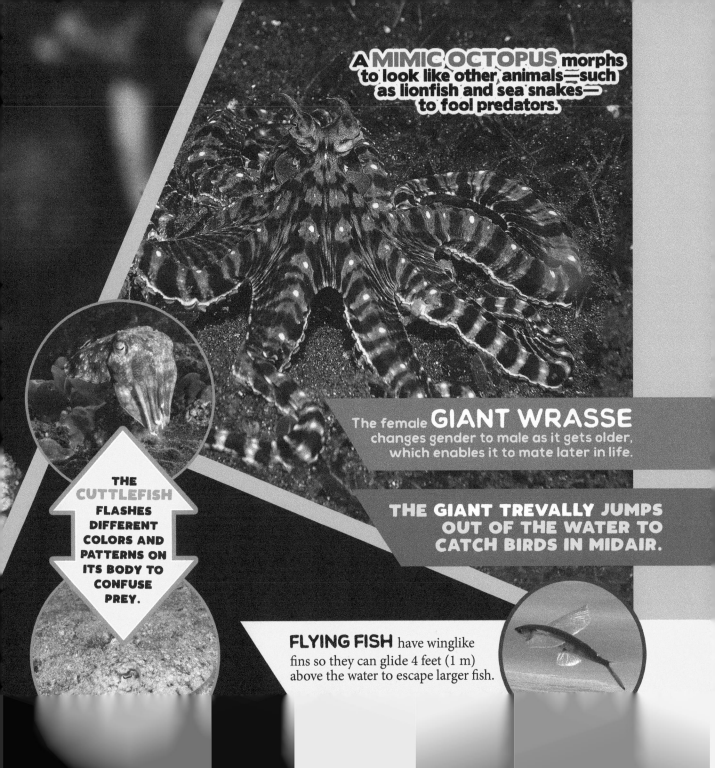

A **MIMIC OCTOPUS** morphs to look like other animals—such as lionfish and sea snakes—to fool predators.

The female **GIANT WRASSE** changes gender to male as it gets older, which enables it to mate later in life.

THE GIANT TREVALLY JUMPS OUT OF THE WATER TO CATCH BIRDS IN MIDAIR.

THE **CUTTLEFISH** FLASHES DIFFERENT COLORS AND PATTERNS ON ITS BODY TO CONFUSE PREY.

FLYING FISH have winglike fins so they can glide 4 feet (1 m) above the water to escape larger fish.

HORSES
OF THE SEA

SEAHORSE DADS ARE ALSO MOMS! THE MALE CARRIES HIS DEVELOPING EGGS UNTIL THEY HATCH.

THE GOLDEN LEAFY SEA DRAGON is so perfectly camouflaged that it has no predators.

SUPER STARFISH

Some species of STARFISH, also called sea stars, can be cut into pieces, and each arm will grow a new starfish.

STARFISH CAN SEE WITH THEIR ARMS— THEY HAVE AN EYESPOT AT THE END OF EACH ONE.

A STARFISH EATS WITH ITS STOMACH OUTSIDE ITS BODY.

LOOK WHO'S SHELLFISH

GIANT CLAMS
are large enough for
a human child to
fit inside.

Unlike mussels and
clams, **SCALLOPS**
can swim by quickly
opening and closing
their shells.

Mussels have beards.
The "beard," or
BYSSUS threads,
keeps the mussel firmly
attached to a surface.

IT TAKES AN OYSTER THREE
YEARS OR MORE TO MAKE A
JEWELRY-SIZED PEARL.

CHAPTER 4

SCALY THINGS

REPTILES ARE NEVER SLIMY. THEIR SCALES ARE OFTEN SMOOTH TO THE TOUCH.

127

SEE YOU LATER, CROC—OR GATOR!

American alligator

IN 1935, AN ALLIGATOR WAS DISCOVERED CLIMBING OUT OF A NEW YORK SEWER.

THE AMERICAN ALLIGATOR AND THE CHINESE ALLIGATOR ARE THE ONLY ALLIGATOR SPECIES IN THE WORLD.

The word **ALLIGATOR** comes from the Spanish word for "the lizard"— **EL LAGARTO.**

CROCODILES CAN'T SWEAT, SO THEY OPEN THEIR MOUTHS TO COOL OFF.

CROCODILES can't chew, so they spin prey underwater in a move called a "death roll" to tear off chunks they can swallow.

THE GHARIAL'S LONG, SKINNY SNOUT IS FILLED WITH OVER 100 TEETH—PERFECT FOR SNAPPING UP FISH.

THE ONE AND ONLY TUATARA

The tuatara is the only survivor of a group of reptiles that lived about 200 million years ago.

The tuatara has a small, sightless third eye on top of its head.

129

GIANT LIZARDS

The **MARINE IGUANA** is the only lizard that lives its whole life in the water.

THE RHINOCEROS IGUANA

looks fierce, but its horns are actually just very large scales.

GILA MONSTERS, KOMODO DRAGONS, AND BEADED LIZARDS ARE ALL VENOMOUS.

Gila monster

A NILE MONITOR USES ITS LONG TAIL TO STEER WHILE SWIMMING AND TO WHACK PREDATORS.

The 10-foot-long (2.1-m) **KOMODO DRAGON** can eat 80 percent of its body weight in one meal. That is like a 50-pound (23-kg) kid eating 160 hamburgers.

Komodo dragon

SCALES AND SPIKES

A **THORNY DEVIL** CAN EAT 2,500 ANTS IN ONE MEAL.

The **HORNED LIZARD** has a truly bizarre skill. It shoots blood out of its eyes!

THE ARMADILLO LIZARD DEFENDS ITSELF BY ROLLING INTO A SPIKY BALL AND HOLDING ITS TAIL IN ITS MOUTH.

BEARDED DRAGONS can change their beard colors to communicate.

LEAPIN' LIZARDS

THE MALE AGAMA IS BROWN, BUT IT BURSTS INTO COLOR DURING MATING SEASON.

Agama

THE BASILISK CAN RUN ACROSS WATER ON TWO LEGS.

The **LEOPARD GECKO**'s tail expands to store extra fat, then shrinks as its body uses up the fat.

THE MALE **GREEN ANOLE** PUFFS OUT HIS CHIN AND DOES TINY PUSHUPS TO SHOW OTHERS HOW BIG AND TOUGH HE IS.

THE FLYING LIZARD USES ITS SKIN FOLDS TO GLIDE BETWEEN TREES WHILE STEERING WITH ITS TAIL.

LEGLESS LIZARD

A **GLASS LIZARD** LOOKS LIKE A SNAKE, BUT IT IS A LIZARD WITH AN EXTRA-LONG TAIL—AND NO LEGS.

SOMETHING SKINKS

The **FIVE-LINED SKINK** can detach its tail to distract a predator—the tail even wiggles like a snake for a while!

THE **STUMP-TAILED SKINK'S TAIL LOOKS LIKE ITS HEAD, SO PREDATORS DON'T KNOW WHICH END TO GRAB.**

Five-lined skink

THE BLUE-TONGUED SKINK
has—surprise!—a long blue tongue.

COLORFUL CHAMELEONS

A CHAMELEON'S TONGUE IS TWICE THE LENGTH OF ITS BODY.

A CHAMELEON'S tongue can flick **62 MILES** (100 km) per hour in 0.01 second.

138

PANTHER CHAMELEONS CHANGE COLORS TO REFLECT THEIR MOOD, NOT TO CAMOUFLAGE THEMSELVES.

A male JACKSON'S CHAMELEON looks like a tiny TRICERATOPS and uses its bony horns to fight other males.

The tiny LEAF CHAMELEON can fit on the tip of your finger.

A **RATTLESNAKE** shakes its famous tail-tip **RATTLE** to tell a predator to back off.

Rattlesnake

A **BOOMSLANG** CAN BE MISTAKEN FOR A TREE BRANCH—UNTIL IT STRIKES, FAST AND FIERCE.

THE INLAND TAIPAN'S VENOM PARALYZES ITS PREY ALMOST INSTANTLY.

THE DEATH ADDER vibrates the tip of its pale tail like an insect in the grass to **LURE PREY CLOSER.**

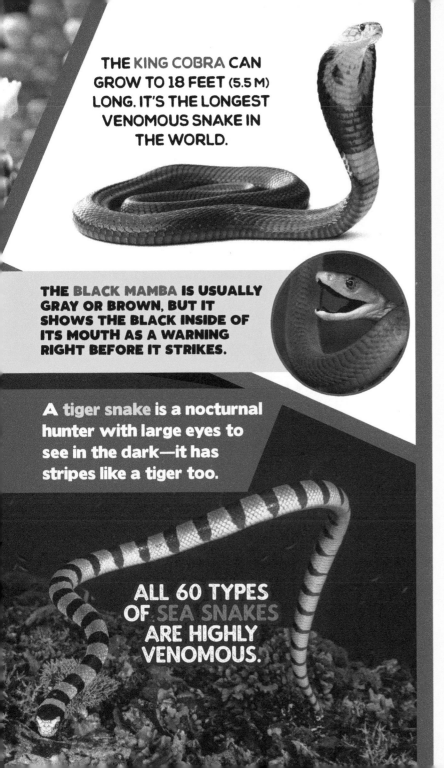

THE KING COBRA CAN GROW TO 18 FEET (5.5 M) LONG. IT'S THE LONGEST VENOMOUS SNAKE IN THE WORLD.

THE BLACK MAMBA IS USUALLY GRAY OR BROWN, BUT IT SHOWS THE BLACK INSIDE OF ITS MOUTH AS A WARNING RIGHT BEFORE IT STRIKES.

A tiger snake is a nocturnal hunter with large eyes to see in the dark—it has stripes like a tiger too.

ALL 60 TYPES OF SEA SNAKES ARE HIGHLY VENOMOUS.

POISON VS. VENOM

POISON is inside an animal's body and delivered when another animal eats or touches it.

VENOM is injected into another animal through biting or stinging.

AN **EMERALD TREE BOA**'S BABIES ARE RED, ORANGE, OR YELLOW. THEY CHANGE TO GREEN AT ABOUT ONE YEAR OLD.

Emerald tree boa

THE GREEN ANACONDA weighs 550 pounds (250 kg) and is capable of swallowing an alligator.

THE RETICULATED PYTHON
IS THE WORLD'S LONGEST SNAKE. IT CAN GROW TO MORE THAN 48 FEET (14 M) LONG.

Reticulated python

CONSTRICTORS KILL BY SQUEEZING THEIR PREY UNTIL ITS HEART STOPS BEATING.

Albino boa constrictor

143

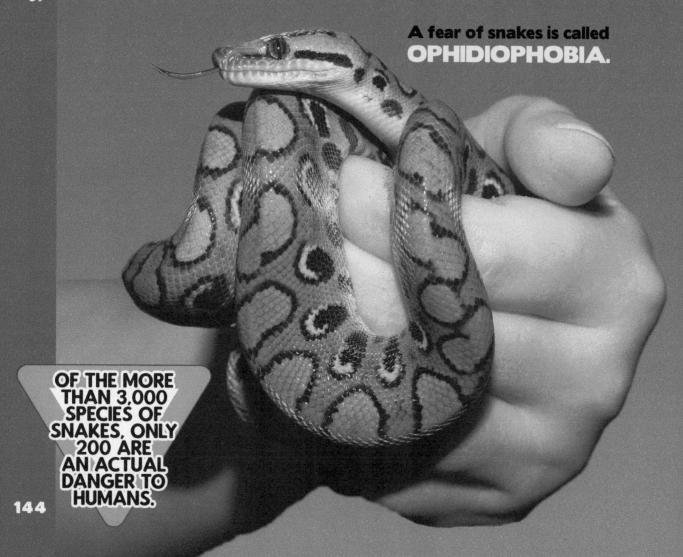

SCARED OF SNAKES?

A fear of snakes is called
OPHIDIOPHOBIA.

OF THE MORE THAN 3,000 SPECIES OF SNAKES, ONLY 200 ARE AN ACTUAL DANGER TO HUMANS.

SUPER-SPECIAL SNAKES

SOME SNAKES ARE ALBINO: WHITE WITH RED EYES. AND WHILE IT'S EVEN MORE RARE, SOME SNAKES HAVE TWO HEADS.

SNAKE TRICKS

A HOGNOSE SNAKE often plays dead. When threatened, it flops over, sticks out its tongue, and squirts a stinky liquid.

Kingsnake

Coral snake

THE HARMLESS KINGSNAKE FOOLS ITS ENEMIES BY MIMICKING THE DEADLY CORAL SNAKE'S COLORS.

146

TURTLE
TEETH

TURTLES AND TORTOISES DO NOT HAVE TEETH; THEY HAVE HARD BEAKS LIKE BIRDS.

BOYS OR GIRLS?

For many turtle species—and alligators, too—**FEMALES** hatch from eggs that are kept **WARMER**, while **MALES** hatch from eggs that are kept **COOLER**.

SEA TURTLES

GREEN TURTLES EAT SO MUCH ALGAE AND SEA GRASS THAT THEIR CARTILAGE AND FAT ARE BOTH GREEN.

Young HAWKSBILL SEA TURTLES eat mostly sponges and jellyfish. Their beaks are shaped to make grabbing sponges from crevices easy.

Green turtle

LEATHERBACK SEA TURTLES HAVE SMOOTH, RUBBER-LIKE SHELLS.

RIVER DWELLERS

THE ALLIGATOR SNAPPING TURTLE wiggles a wormlike part on its tongue to lure fish to its mouth.

A SNAKE-NECKED TURTLE's neck can be longer than its body.

THE **MATAMATA** USES ITS POINTY SNOUT LIKE A SNORKEL TO BREATHE AIR WHILE UNDERWATER.

LAND TURTLES

GALÁPAGOS TORTOISES FACE OFF WITH THEIR MOUTHS OPEN WHEN THERE IS A DISPUTE. THE HIGHER HEAD WINS!

THE COMMON BOX TURTLE CAN PULL ITS ENTIRE BODY INSIDE ITS SHELL AND SHUT IT TIGHTLY LIKE A BOX.

A LEOPARD TORTOISE's bumpy, spotted shell protects it from becoming prey and keeps it cool.

Galápagos tortoise

THE MASSIVE GALÁPAGOS TORTOISE CAN LIVE MORE THAN 100 YEARS.

CHAPTER 5
AMAZING AMPHIBIANS

THE WORD AMPHIBIAN MEANS "BOTH LIVES" IN GREEK BECAUSE MOST START THEIR LIVES IN WATER AND THEN LIVE ON LAND.

SALAMANDERS VS. NEWTS

A NEWT IS A TYPE OF SALAMANDER THAT LIVES MOST OF ITS LIFE IN WATER.

SMILING AXOLOTL

AXOLOTLS DON'T CHANGE MUCH AS THEY GROW AND, UNLIKE OTHER SALAMANDERS, THEY NEVER LOSE THEIR GILLS.

The **AXOLOTL** lives only in Lake Xochimilco, Mexico, and is almost extinct in the wild.

AXOLOTLS can be brown, black, gray, gold, pink, or white. Some even have spots.

THE AXOLOTL is also called a **WALKING FISH.**

WHAT'S IN A NAME?

The **HELLBENDER** is also called a snot otter, because it is covered with a mucus-like substance.

A **GREATER SIREN** doesn't make an alarm sound, but it can click and yelp.

The greater siren can survive a two-year drought by burying itself in mud.

THE **SIREN** IS NAMED AFTER THE SIRENS IN GREEK MYTHOLOGY—MYSTERIOUS WOMEN WHOSE BEAUTIFUL SINGING LURED SAILORS TO THEIR ISLAND. OUTSIDE WATER THEY MADE A YELPING SOUND.

THE **MUDPUPPY** HAS FRILLY RED GILLS FOR ITS ENTIRE LIFE.

Mudpuppies make a squeaky whine that some people say sounds like a dog.

157

IN THE DARK

THE OLM IS A SALAMANDER THAT LIVES IN DARK CAVES. ITS TINY EYES CAN ONLY SENSE LIGHT.

COLORFUL CHARACTERS

SOME YOUNG TIGER SALAMANDER LARVAE ARE CANNIBALS AND EAT THEIR SIBLINGS.

THE RED SALAMANDER IS EASY TO CONFUSE WITH THE RED EFT.

Red salamander

THE FIRE SALAMANDER squirts a toxic liquid to tell predators to stay away.

THE MANDARIN NEWT'S SCIENTIFIC NAME INCLUDES THE WORD SHANJING, WHICH IS MANDARIN FOR "MOUNTAIN DEMON."

159

FROG

Frogs have smooth skin, while most toads are rough and bumpy.

Frogs live both in water and on land, while most toads live mainly on land.

Frogs have tiny teeth. Toads don't have any.

VS.

They both swallow their food whole.

Both frogs and toads have to close their eyes in order to swallow food.

160

TOAD

BIG BOYS

African bullfrog

AFRICAN BULLFROG MALES GROW LONG TOOTHLIKE STRUCTURES IN THEIR LOWER JAWS TO USE IN FIGHTS WITH OTHER MALES.

The male **GOLIATH FROG** weighs about 7 pounds (3,200 g)— about as much as a **HUMAN BABY.**

161

IT'S NOT EASY BEING GREEN

THE GLASS FROG HAS SKIN SO THIN THAT YOU CAN SEE ITS INSIDES— AND EVEN WATCH ITS HEART BEATING.

Glass frog

KERMIT THE FROG is supposed to be from Louisiana, but he looks just like the glass frog, which is native to Costa Rica.

STARTING OVER

FROGS regularly shed their skin—and then gobble it up.

IF A NEWT LOSES OR DAMAGES A LEG, IT CAN GROW A NEW ONE.

UP IN THE TREES

RED-EYED TREE FROGS lay their eggs on the bottoms of leaves that hang above water. When the tadpoles hatch, they drop into the water.

THE CHUBBY-LOOKING WHITE'S TREE FROG HAS EXTRA-LARGE STICKY PADS ON ITS TOES FOR CLIMBING.

GREEN TREE FROGS OFTEN CLIMB UP HOUSE WALLS TO STALK INSECTS BUZZING AROUND LIGHTS AT NIGHT.

TINY TERRORS

THERE ARE MORE THAN 100 SPECIES OF POISON DART FROGS, ALL BRIGHTLY COLORED.

AMAZON RAINFOREST NATIVES HAVE BEEN KNOWN TO DIP THEIR BLOWGUN DART TIPS IN THE FROG'S POISON TO INSTANTLY KILL ANIMALS HIGH IN THE TREES.

POISON DART FROGS ARE THE MOST POISONOUS ANIMALS. EATING—OR SOMETIMES LICKING—ONE CAUSES ALMOST INSTANT DEATH.

A GOLDEN POISON DART FROG is only about 1 inch (2.5 cm) long, but its poison can kill 10 people.

TIME FOR SPRING

MALE **SPRING PEEPERS** GATHER AT THE BEGINNING OF SPRING, PUFF OUT THEIR THROAT SACS, AND WHISTLE LOUDLY TO ATTRACT FEMALES.

FLYING HIGH

THE WALLACE'S FLYING FROG spreads out its large, webbed toes like a parachute and glides 50 feet (15.2 m) between trees.

THE BIG FREEZE

THE WOOD FROG IS THE ONLY FROG THAT LIVES IN THE ARCTIC CIRCLE.

While the **WOOD FROG** is frozen, its breathing, blood flow, and heartbeat **ALL STOP.**

This **FROG** freezes solid in winter and then thaws in the spring. Its body makes a substance like **ANTIFREEZE**, which helps it survive being frozen.

WARNING: BACK OFF!

WHEN THREATENED, THE FIRE-BELLIED TOAD **CAN FLIP OVER TO REVEAL ITS BRIGHT BELLY AND THEN OOZE POISON.**

Fire-bellied toad

THE COMMON TOAD PUFFS OUT ITS BODY TO DISPLAY ITS WARTY SKIN AND LOOK AS BIG AS POSSIBLE.

THE FOUR-EYED FROG TURNS AROUND TO REVEAL CONFUSING FAKE EYES ON ITS REAR END.

BABY TALK

The female **MARSUPIAL FROG** carries her babies in a pouch like a kangaroo, but the pouch is on her back.

THE PARADOXICAL **FROG TADPOLE** IS ABOUT THREE TIMES THE SIZE OF ITS PARENTS, BUT IT SHRINKS AS IT AGES.

Marsupial frog

BABY SURINAM TOADS HATCH OUT OF THEIR MOTHER'S BACK.

The male Darwin's frog keeps his mate's newly hatched tadpoles safe—in his throat—until they are ready to go out on their own.

THE MALE MIDWIFE TOAD WRAPS HIS MATE'S EGGS AROUND HIS LEGS AND CARRIES THEM UNTIL THEY HATCH.

169

CANE TOADS
TAKE OVER

In 1935, about **100 CANE TOADS** were brought to Australia to eat **SUGARCANE BEETLES.** The toads ate everything in sight, and now there may be more than **1 BILLION** of them in the country.

CHAPTER 6

FEATHERED FRIENDS

BIRDS ARE THE ONLY LIVING CREATURES ON EARTH WITH FEATHERS.

THE AWARD GOES TO . . .

LARGEST: The ostrich can be up to 9 feet (2.7 m) tall. It is also the fastest runner, reaching speeds of 45 miles (72 km) per hour, and sometimes even faster for short periods of time.

FASTEST DIVER: THE PEREGRINE FALCON CAN REACH 240 MILES (386 KM) PER HOUR WHEN DIVING FOR PREY.

STRONGEST: The harpy eagle can carry a 15-pound (6.8-kg) monkey in its talons while flying.

LARGEST WINGSPAN: THE ALBATROSS'S WINGS CAN REACH 12 FEET (3.7 M) ACROSS.

SMALLEST: THE BEE HUMMINGBIRD IS ABOUT 2 INCHES (51 MM) LONG AND ITS WINGS BEAT 90 TIMES PER SECOND— UP TO 200 WHEN IT'S MATING!

BIG BIRD

AN OSTRICH'S LEGS
ARE SO STRONG THAT
A WELL-PLACED KICK
CAN KILL A LION.

AN OSTRICH'S EYES
ARE EACH BIGGER
THAN ITS BRAIN.

The **OSTRICH** is
the only two-toed bird.

FLIGHTLESS BIRDS

THE COLORFUL CASSOWARY HAS A SCALY BLUE FACE AND A FLOPPY RED NECK. IT LAYS LARGE GREEN EGGS.

Emus can't fly, but they can jump 7 feet (2.1 m) straight into the air.

PEOPLE FROM NEW ZEALAND ARE CALLED KIWIS AFTER THEIR NATIONAL BIRD—THE FLIGHTLESS KIWI.

175

BEAKS AND BILLS

The **PILEATED WOODPECKER** hammers a hole into a tree, then uses its sticky tongue to grab termites.

The SWORD-BILLED HUMMINGBIRD'S beak is about 4 inches (10.2 cm) long—longer than the rest of its tiny body.

THE ATLANTIC PUFFIN'S BIG BEAK IS COLORFUL DURING THE BREEDING SEASON AND DULL IN WINTER.

THE SHOEBILL USES ITS BILL, LIKE SCISSORS, TO CUT ITS FOOD BEFORE EATING IT.

The TOCO TOUCAN's large beak looks HEAVY, but since it's hollow, it is VERY LIGHT.

A ROSEATE SPOONBILL SWINGS ITS BILL FROM SIDE TO SIDE IN THE WATER, FEELING FOR PREY, THEN SNAPPING IT UP.

177

FLAMBOYANT FLAMINGOS

FLAMINGO FEATHERS GET THEIR PINK, PEACH, OR RED COLOR FROM THE SHRIMP AND ALGAE THE BIRD EATS.

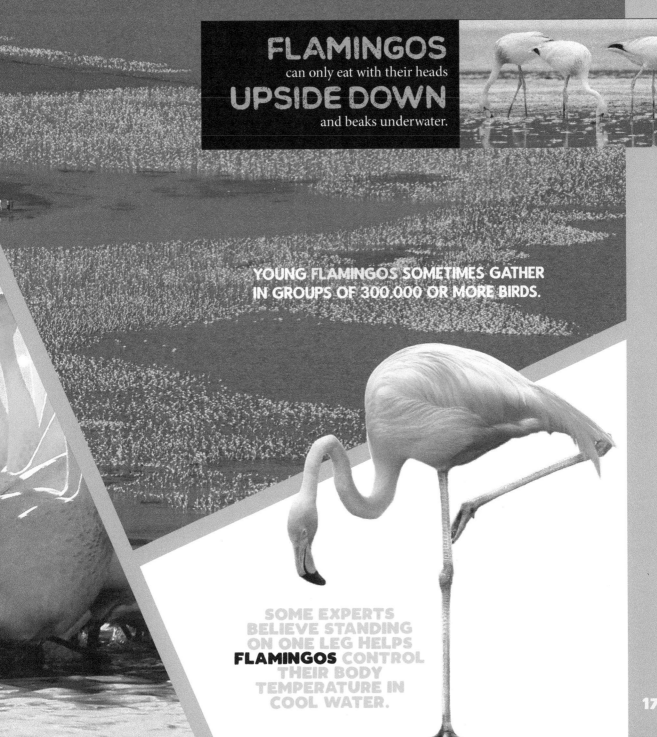

FLAMINGOS can only eat with their heads **UPSIDE DOWN** and beaks underwater.

YOUNG FLAMINGOS SOMETIMES GATHER IN GROUPS OF 300,000 OR MORE BIRDS.

SOME EXPERTS BELIEVE STANDING ON ONE LEG HELPS **FLAMINGOS** CONTROL THEIR BODY TEMPERATURE IN COOL WATER.

IMPRESSIVE MALES WITH
PRETTY TAILS

WITH ITS 6-FOOT-LONG (1.8-M) TAIL FEATHERS, THE MALE **PEACOCK** IS ONE OF THE LARGEST BIRDS THAT CAN FLY.

THE **RESPLENDENT QUETZAL'S** TAIL FEATHERS ARE OFTEN LONGER THAN THE REST OF ITS BODY.

THE MALE **SUPERB LYREBIRD** SINGS, DANCES, AND SHAKES HIS TAIL FEATHERS TO ATTRACT FEMALES.

GOBBLE, GOBBLE, WHAT?

THE SOUND A **TURKEY** MAKES IN ENGLISH IS GOBBLE GOBBLE, BUT IN FRANCE AND GREECE IT'S *GLOU GLOU*, IN SPAIN IT'S *CLOU CLOU*, AND IN MEXICO IT'S *GORO GORO*.

FIRST BIRD

ARCHAEOPTERYX (ARK-EE-OP-TUR-ICKS), MEANING "ANCIENT WING," IS ONE OF THE FIRST BIRDS THAT EVER LIVED.

Archaeopteryx fossil

MOST SCIENTISTS TODAY AGREE THAT BIRDS ARE NOT JUST DINOSAUR RELATIVES, THEY *ARE* MODERN-DAY DINOSAURS.

ROYAL BIRDS

Queen Elizabeth owns all the unmarked mute swans in England, and she has a Royal Swan warden who keeps track of them.

Legend says that the **TOWER OF LONDON** must contain six **RAVENS** or England will fall to its enemies, so six ravens (plus one spare) are always kept there—and they're members of the **BRITISH ARMY.**

182

BIRDS WITH JOBS

Some **CORMORANTS** have been trained to catch fish and bring them back to **FISHERMEN.**

Golden eagle

IN THE PAST, RAVENS AND PIGEONS WERE TRAINED TO BE SPIES FOR THE CIA.

GOLDEN EAGLES ARE TRAINED FOR SEVERAL YEARS TO HUNT AND RETURN THEIR KILL TO THEIR TRAINERS.

NIFTY NESTS

OROPENDOLAS BUILD LONG, TEARDROP-SHAPED NESTS IN THE TALL RAINFOREST TREES.

In his nest, the male **BOWERBIRD** displays insects, stones, flowers, or other items he collects to attract females.

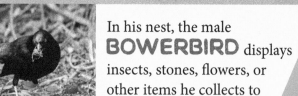

A **BALD EAGLE**'s nest, called an aerie, can weigh **ONE TON**.

184

SOCIABLE WEAVER BIRDS CREATE GIANT NESTS IN ACACIA TREES WITH UP TO 100 CHAMBERS—ONE FOR EACH MATED PAIR OF BIRDS.

Weaver bird

Malleefowl

MALLEEFOWL
nests can be 3.3 feet (1 m) tall and 16 feet (5 m) wide.

ON THE MOVE

ARCTIC TERNS have the longest migration, flying an incredible **44,000 MILES** (70,800 km) each year.

WHY DO CANADA GEESE FLY IN A V SHAPE? FLYING BEHIND ANOTHER BIRD HELPS THEM CONSERVE ENERGY ON THEIR LONG JOURNEY AND KNOW THAT EVERYONE IS ACCOUNTED FOR.

The
SOOTY TERN
can fly constantly for
years, napping
only seconds
at a time.

RUBY-THROATED
HUMMINGBIRDS MIGRATE
500 MILES (805 KM), FROM FLORIDA
TO THE YUCATAN, IN JUST 22 HOURS.

BIRD TOWNS

These US town
names are
for the birds!

Flamingo, Florida

Parrott, Georgia

Pelican, Louisiana

Eagle, Nebraska

Turkey, Texas

White Swan, Washington

Turkey, Texas

187

TRICKY BIRDS

Clark's nutcracker

THE CLARK'S NUTCRACKER HIDES MORE THAN 30,000 SEEDS TO RETRIEVE AND EAT DURING WINTER—AND REMEMBERS WHERE MOST OF THEM ARE.

The **Egyptian plover** picks out the leftover food from between crocodiles' teeth.

HERRING GULLS WILL DROP SHELLFISH FROM HIGH IN THE AIR TO SHATTER THE SHELLS AND GET TO THE MEAT INSIDE.

The **EGYPTIAN VULTURE** eats ostrich eggs. It throws stones at the eggs to break them open.

Some wild **COCKATOOS** use twigs as drumsticks to play catchy beats on hollow trees as a mating technique.

189

BIRD TALK

The **COMMON LOON** has a famous wailing cry that sounds like a howling wolf.

Baby western gulls can warn each other of danger before hatching—from inside their eggs.

THE NORTHERN MOCKINGBIRD CAN IMITATE OTHER BIRDS' CALLS, BARKING DOGS, AND EVEN CAR ALARMS.

ROADRUNNERS MAKE A COOING NOISE THAT SOUNDS LIKE A CAT PURRING.

THE KOOKABURRA'S CACKLING CALL MAKES THE BIRD SOUND LIKE IT JUST HEARD THE BEST JOKE EVER.

191

OUTSTANDING OWLS

THE GREAT HORNED OWL IS SUCH AN EXCELLENT HUNTER THAT IT IS NICKNAMED THE "TIGER OWL."

A female **BURROWING OWL** digs a long tunnel or takes over another animal's burrow and makes a large chamber for laying her eggs.

THE SNOWY OWL

nests on the ground because there are no trees in the

ARCTIC TUNDRA.

SPECIAL FEATHERS ON OWLS' WINGS MAKE THEIR FLIGHT ALMOST TOTALLY SILENT, SO THEY CAN SURPRISE PREY.

THE EASTERN SCREECH OWL BRINGS BLIND SNAKES TO HER NEST TO EAT INSECTS THAT COULD HARM HER CHICKS.

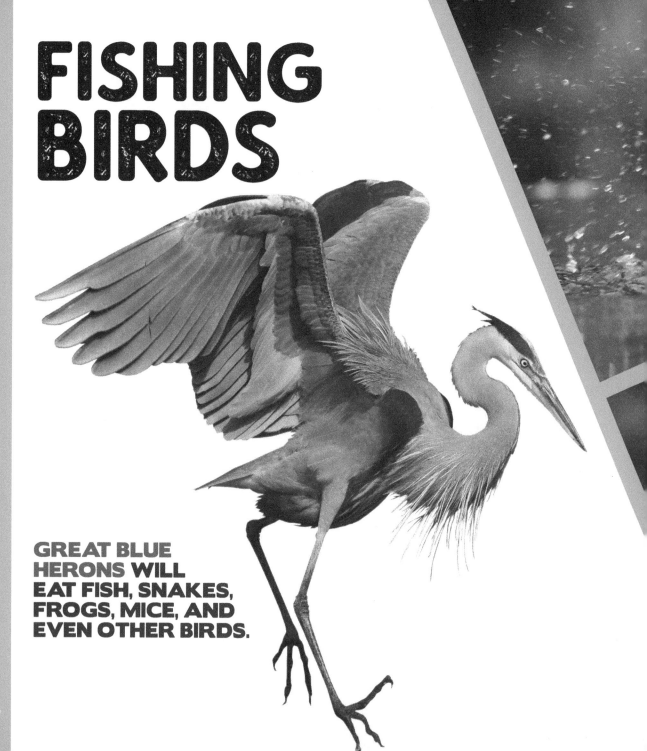

FISHING BIRDS

GREAT BLUE HERONS WILL EAT FISH, SNAKES, FROGS, MICE, AND EVEN OTHER BIRDS.

THE AMAZON KINGFISHER'S HEAD IS SO AERODYNAMIC THAT SOME JAPANESE HIGH-SPEED TRAINS ARE MODELED AFTER ITS SHAPE.

THE AUSTRALIAN PELICAN'S POUCH IS POROUS ENOUGH TO LET WATER DRAIN THROUGH, LEAVING FISH BEHIND.

OSPREYS point their prey forward to reduce wind resistance when flying.

A WADDLE OF PENGUINS

MACARONI PENGUINS HOP ON BOTH FEET INSTEAD OF **WADDLING** LIKE MOST PENGUINS.

ALL PENGUIN SPECIES LIVE IN THE SOUTHERN HEMISPHERE, BUT SOME GALÁPAGOS PENGUINS ALSO LIVE IN THE NORTHERN HEMISPHERE.

EMPEROR PENGUINS CAN DIVE UP TO 1,750 FEET (530 M)— THAT'S MORE THAN A QUARTER OF A MILE (.4 KM).

EMPEROR PENGUINS ARE ABOUT THE SAME HEIGHT AS A SIX-YEAR-OLD HUMAN.

DO ALL PENGUINS LIVE IN COLD PLACES? NO, AFRICAN PENGUINS LIVE ON THE SOUTH AFRICAN COAST.

THEY'RE CALLED WHAT?!

WATCH OUT! A GROUP OF CROWS IS CALLED A MURDER.

A group of starlings is called a murmuration because they sound like many people murmuring.

Plovers gathered together are a congregation—like people sitting quietly in a church.

A bunch of owls is a parliament—like the legislature in Britain. *Whooo* put them in charge?

A GROUP OF EAGLES FORMS A CONVOCATION—WHICH IS A FORMAL CEREMONY LIKE A COLLEGE GRADUATION.

198

Peacocks **are so fancy they're called an ostentation—a display meant to impress others.**

LARKS FLYING TOGETHER MAKE AN EXALTATION, WHICH ALSO MEANS "A FEELING OF EXTREME HAPPINESS."

PARROTS FORM A PANDEMONIUM— OR AN UPROAR OF NOISE AND CONFUSION.

199

Ginjer L. Clarke lives in Richmond, Virginia, with her husband, son, and several silly pets. She loves being outdoors, hiking and kayaking, but she's also happy inside, reading and baking. She enjoys traveling to schools to give author presentations, but staying home researching cool science stuff and writing in her pajamas is her dream job. She is the author of 25 picture books, beginner readers, and chapter books. Find out more about Ginjer on her website, GinjerClarkeBooks.com, and on Facebook, Instagram, or Twitter: @GinjerClarkeBooks.

CPSIA information can be obtained
at www.ICGtesting.com
Printed in the USA
JSHW031041260320
4886JS00001B/1

9 781646 111497